PREDIABETES PLAN AND COOKBOOK

Your Complete Guide to Reverse Prediabetes (Includes a 7-Day Meal Plan)

Nancy Peterson

Copyright@2019

TABLE OF CONTENT

Introduction 4
Chapter One 8
Understanding Prediabetes 8
Testing for Prediabetes 12
Myths about Prediabetes and Diabetes .. 16
Causes of Prediabetes 36
Risk Factors of Prediabetes 37
Ways to Fight, Prevent and Reverse Prediabetes 40
Foods to Limit When Treating/ Preventing Prediabetic 46
Health Implications of Prediabetes 48
Chapter Two 55
Explaining Diabetes 55
Type of Diabetes 58
Chapter Three 70
Setting up a Diet Plan 70
Types of Diet 72

A 7-Day 1,200 Calories (per day) Meal Plan. 82

Chapter Four 94

Prediabetes Friendly Recipes 94

Chapter 5 172

Conclusion 172

Other Books by Nancy Peterson 174

Introduction

As common among us as the oxygen we share, prediabetes is a medical condition that has been plaguing millions of people around the globe. The name "prediabetes" is a recently adopted label for this long-existing condition in the medical world. Just like HIV is the "pre-AIDS" stage, Prediabetes is the "pre-Diabetes" stage.

The similarity here is that these diseases have a preceding stage but the difference is that unlike HIV, prediabetes can be reversed. As the name suggests, it is a condition that occurs in the human body before Type 2 Diabetes set in. It is ranked as one of the most common chronic illness, just second to Obesity.

In the United States of America alone, the prevalent rate of people with this condition is nearly triple the rate of those diagnosed with Diabetes. With a staggering approximate of 84 million adults being diagnosed with prediabetes, it gives a glimpse of the presence of this condition in other parts of the world, mostly among the adult population.

This statistic means that 1 out of every 3 adults in America is prediabetic. An absolute majority of this vast number have no idea that they are prediabetic.

So, what is prediabetes? It is a health condition in which the blood sugar level of people spikes above the normal region but not high enough to be termed diabetes. In other words, it occurs in people with very high blood sugar than is healthy but not high enough to be called diabetes.

However, be comforted that it is not too late to control and reverse the condition as long as you got tested and found out the prediabetic condition on time. All you need to do is make some certain changes to your lifestyle like change of diet, losing excess fat, maintaining a healthy weight, increase in physical exercises and regular exercises.

In this book, we would look at what causes prediabetes, the symptoms and how to reverse/ prevent it via exercise and right diet.

Chapter One

Understanding Prediabetes

How this condition develops in the body shouldn't be a mystery. When the insulin is not utilized or produced adequately by the body, it causes an unhealthy accumulation of glucose in the blood, which automatically spikes up your blood sugar level to the range of prediabetes. If you do not take the right measures to control and reverse it, it then turns to full blown diabetes. Prediabetes is also known as Impaired Fasting Glucose (IFG), Borderline Diabetes and Impaired Glucose Tolerance (IGT).

According to data sourced from the American Diabetes Association, before one can be termed prediabetic, there has to be an escalated fasting blood glucose level (100mg/dL – 125mg/dL) i.e. 100-125 milligram per decilitre, a glycated haemoglobin measurement of 5.7% to 6.4% or an escalated blood sugar level after undergoing glucose tolerance test taken orally (140 – 199mg/dL).

According to data sourced from the National Diabetes Statistics Report, a total approximate of 84.1 million Americans aged 18 years and above are prediabetic. This is approximately 34% percent of the adult population of America. As for a more advanced age segment of the population, precisely 65 years of age and above, approximately 23.1 million of individuals in this age bracket are prediabetic.

If you are diagnosed with prediabetes, it doesn't mean that you automatically have the more serious case which is diabetes, it is only a warning that if you do not handle the condition then it can turn to type 2 diabetes. A prediabetic patient has a higher risk of developing diabetes than someone who isn't prediabetic. One has to have prediabetes before you can be diagnosed of diabetes. Unfortunately, several people do not get tested on time and so do not know of their prediabetic condition before it explodes to the type 2 diabetes. Apart from a high risk of developing diabetes, you also tend to have high risks of contracting other severe and lethal health complications, such as stroke and heart disease.

If you experience the symptoms below, you should ensure to test for prediabetes:

- You get abnormally thirsty
- Frequent visit to the loo for a leak more times than is usual
- Blurry sight
- High level of exhaustion and fatigue.

Although these symptoms are not particular to the prediabetic status, it is important you do the necessary tests for your peace of mind and for proper treatment if tested positive.

Prediabetes are mostly common with adults from the age of 45 upwards and people who are overweight. If you are within this age bracket, it is important that you get tested as often as possible.

Testing for Prediabetes

There are multiple tests that can be used to diagnose if a person has this condition or not. It reveals your blood sugar level, and you get to know which level you are in. There are three levels indicated from the outcome of the test;

- Normal
- Prediabetic
- Diabetic.

If your result indicates a blood sugar level that is below 100 milligrams per decilitre (mg/dL), it means you are normal and healthy. If your result indicates a blood sugar level of between 100 to125 milligrams per decilitre (mg/dL), it means you are prediabetic. If your result indicates a blood sugar level of 126 and above milligrams per decilitre, after repeat tests are done to be absolutely certain, it means you have the big D. You are diabetic.

Fasting Blood Glucose Test

The sugar level in our body is not fixed, it goes up or down while maintaining a normal range. To do this test, you have to abstain from food for minimum of 8 hours before the blood sugar test is conducted. Once the result is ready, you would use the reading above to know your health status.

Oral Glucose Tolerance Test

This test is similar to the fasting blood sugar test with an additional requirement.

First is to avoid any food for a minimum of 8 hours after which you need to drink any sweet liquid preferably carbonated drinks or any drink that has about 75grams of sugar.

Your blood sugar level would be checked before you take the drink, a second test would be done an hour after you take the drink then a third test would be taken two hours after. If your blood sugar test reads between 144-190mg/dL after the 3rd test conducted 2 hours later, this means you are prediabetic.

Haemoglobin A1C

For this test type, you do not need to avoid food for any period of time. This test type simply checks your average blood sugar level for the past two to three months. It is also called glycohemoglobin and glycated haemoglobin test. Haemoglobin is simply protein in the red blood cells.

Result of this test will look exactly like this:

- Normal: below 5.6%
- Prediabetes: 5.7%-6.4%
- Diabetes: 6.5%.

Being diagnosed with prediabetes doesn't mean you would automatically have diabetes. Recent studies show that when a prediabetic patient loses between 5 to 7% of body mass through the right diet and physical fitness exercises, it would reduce the likelihood of having diabetes.

Myths about Prediabetes and Diabetes

The myths and the facts concerning these health conditions will be discussed here. We would first address the myths surrounding prediabetes followed by facts to disprove this myth.

Myth: Prediabetes isn't a big deal

Fact: Don't be fooled by the "pre", prediabetes is a big deal because if it isn't taken seriously, managed and reversed, your certain destination will be Diabetes. Other possible consequences are dreadful illnesses like kidney damage, nerve damage, blood vessels damage, heart diseases, stroke and so on.

Myth: Like other health conditions, Prediabetes will show warning signals or symptoms. It can't go undetected.

Fact: Sorry to burst your bubble but you can be prediabetic for years without knowing. This is because prediabetes has no crystal-clear warning signs and the symptoms commonly associated with it could be the symptoms for a myriad of other illnesses. The surest way to diagnose this condition is by going for a blood sugar test. It is advisable you do the test if you possess any or some of the risk factors associated with having Prediabetes.

Myth: Prediabetes is not Diabetes. It is not a risky condition.

Fact: Sadly, the name might be a euphemism, which puts diagnosed prediabetics at ease, since it isn't full-blown diabetes. Well, the bubble buster is prediabetes is in fact, Diabetes. Prediabetes is actually "Phase 1" of Diabetes. So, if you are not careful, you will be on your way to getting associated with one of the most lethal killers of mankind.

Myth: Diabetes cannot be prevented (Prediabetes)

Fact: Prediabetes is a warning sign that leads to diabetes. It can be prevented and reversed, provided you regularly follow the steps written in this book. The real danger here is ignorance and negligence. Approximately 90% of prediabetics are not aware that they have prediabetes, and because you cannot take on what you have no idea about, you do nothing about the growing level of glucose in your blood, thereby increasing your risk of getting type 2 diabetes.

Myth: Eating Sugar Causes Prediabetes and ultimately, type 2 Diabetes.

Fact: Sugar intake doesn't necessarily or directly trigger Prediabetes. It is the failure of the body to respond as it should, to the secretion of insulin that triggers diabetes.

However, if you do not reduce your intake of sugar, it can be an indirect cause. You will likely become obese, which is one of the possible causes of prediabetes. So, while eating sugar doesn't trigger Prediabetes, eating excess sugar over time and carrying out little or no physical activity to balance your blood glucose level would trigger Prediabetes.

A BMJ study conducted in 2015, revealed that the consumption of one sweetened drink a day raises your risk of getting type 2 diabetes by 18%.

It is advisable to watch what you eat; you may be ingesting more sugar than you actually think. Most snacks and processed foods have varying amounts of processed sugar, so consuming them regularly means regularly boosting your blood sugar level. Excess intake of sugar harms the cell in your pancreas that secretes insulin.

Another study revealed that women who increased their intake of sweetened drink from 1 or below 1 to 1 and above per day only succeed in doubling their risk of having the type 2 diabetes.

Myth: You will surely know if your blood glucose level is above the health radar. (Prediabetes)

Fact: beginning signs of increased blood sugar are so low that it is possible not to notice. That is why it is vital you regularly go for blood tests to know the status of your sugar level.

Myth: Lean people cannot have type 2 diabetes.

Fact: having a healthy weight doesn't guarantee against type 2 diabetes. According to Harvard Health Publications, a survey was carried out on diabetic patients in America, findings revealed 85% of diabetic patients were overweight or obese while the remaining 15% had healthy weights.

A study carried out in 2012 by JAMA, revealed that type 2 diabetics patients with healthy weights are twice likely to die from cardiovascular disease and other causes than obese people. Genes could be responsible for this as well as having large amounts of visceral fat, that is, fat that sticks to your abdominal organs. This affects the secretion of the inflammatory compounds which could be harmful to your liver and pancreas, thereby rendering the actions of insulin unproductive in your body.

When you have reached the age 45 years and above, your weight doesn't really matter anymore. It is important you visit your doctor more regularly, especially if you tick the boxes of some of the risk factors that leads to this deadly disease.

Myth: Physical Exercise is harmful for Type 2 Diabetics

Fact: multiple studies have revealed that physical exercises helps manage diabetes because it reduces the blood sugar level.

However, it is vital you consult your doctor before you start exercises, especially if you have been living a sedentary lifestyle. Also enquire, from your doctor the best way to, and the time to test for blood sugar during your fitness activities.

According to Mayo clinic, if you are on medications that can lower blood sugar, ensure you test your blood glucose level thirty minutes before exercising and about thirty minutes after you start your exercises. The essence of doing this is to be aware of your current blood sugar level (whether constant, increasing or reducing). This will help you know if it's safe to stop or continue the exercise.

Myth: You can't detect the symptoms of Type 2 Diabetes. Only your doctor can.

Fact: Actually, there are early warning alarm systems for diabetes but the issue is that despite their presence, they can be easily neglected or taken for granted. This is because they are not harsh symptoms. This is a major reason a good percentage of diabetics are not aware they have the disease.

Watch out for signals such as being dehydrated even after just consuming water, drinking more water than you usually do, higher frequency of urination every day, weight loss despite not changing diet or carrying out any weight loss activity and feeling exhausted always.

If you experience any or some of the above symptoms, please visit your doctor for a blood test. A test is the best way to diagnose diabetes.

Myth: Type 2 Diabetics must follow a diet with complete absence of sugar.

Fact: the key is limiting your intake. Eat more of whole foods, do away with processed foods. Consume lean protein like chicken instead of red meat and consume fruits and vegetables. Reduce your intake of sweetened foods.

Myth: There is no cure for type 2 diabetics.

Fact: type 2 diabetes is the most common form of diabetes in the world. It has always been linked to obesity.

According to Eduardo Sanchez, MD, "the idea of a cure is elusive but it is not outside our grasp", "we are not optimizing our efforts to prevent diabetes and there is a tremendous opportunity for hope because we can dramatically improve quality of life and the length of life of people with diabetes through lifestyle changes and medication".

Myth: All patients with type 2 Diabetes should adhere to the same meal plan.

Fact: According to Dr. Sanchez, there can't possibly be one diet to carry all diabetics along, just like there can't be one meal plan for all non-diabetics.

There are many eating variations that can cater to people with diabetes. There is the Mediterranean diet that is vegetable-rich, lean proteins, whole grains and healthy fats. There is the Keto diet that is high in fat, low in carbohydrates and moderate in protein.

Myth: If you have type 2 Diabetics, you will have heart disease.

Fact: Admittedly, type 2 diabetes leads to serious health complications like nerve damage, kidney damage and of course, heart disease. This doesn't mean if you have diabetes, you are certain to have the above conditions. Medical science has advanced to the stage, where they can effectively lower the risk of diabetics developing such complications and change the course of their condition.

Adopt a lifestyle that is healthy for the heart, make sure your glucose level, cholesterol level and your blood pressure is at a healthy level.

Sensitizing diabetic and non-diabetic patients about the increased risk of developing heart disease for people with type 2 diabetes, goes a long way in getting more people to adopt a healthy lifestyle whether they have the disease or not.

Myth: Type 2 Diabetes will certainly lead to the amputation of a limb.

Fact: According to Maria Rodriguez, "Staying well informed about how to manage blood sugar and taking your medications as directed is the best way to prevent complications such as losing a limb.

To ensure it doesn't come to amputation, schedule a formal foot examination at least once in a year, while you also do some self-checks every day.

Also ensure that as a diabetic patient, you avoid injuries as much as is possible you because any cut on your feet will take a long time to heal. This is because the disease causes nerve damage, which makes your feet insensitive to feel, and limits blood flow to that area.

Myth: Every one with type 2 diabetes needs insulin treatment.

Fact: Insulin treatment applies to some but not all diabetic patients. Other medications, losing weight and exercises can help manage diabetes but in cases where they don't work, insulin therapy would be the next best thing on the agenda.

Myth: Diabetics will surely lose their sight.

Fact: Loss of eyesight is not unstoppable. It can be prevented. Diabetic retinopathy is a common cause of eyesight loss for diabetics. This is because the accumulated blood sugar can destroy the blood vessels in the retina.

Diabetics can prevent losing their eyesight by ensuring they get a complete dilated eye examination at least annually.

Myth: Dialysis is a must for every diabetic.

Fact: type 2 diabetes does lead to kidney damage if not treated and left to become worse. Kidney damage makes the kidney unable to filter the blood in the body and dialysis will need to take over.

However, with efficient management of diabetes by strict blood sugar control, the risk of getting complications such as kidney damage will be significantly reduced.

Myth: Diabetics cannot Consume Alcohol

Fact: This is not true. Even if you have diabetes, you can consume alcohol but it must be in moderate quantity. Being careful is important because alcohol contains some calories that give energy but little or no nutrition, these calories when in the body converts to sugar, then breaks down as fat.

Also, if you want to mix drinks, diet soda will be a better option than sweet drinks. A maximum of one drink per day for female diabetics and two drinks per day for male diabetics.

Also, never consume alcohol on an empty stomach because this escalates the risk of getting low blood sugar. So, empty stomach plus drinking raises your chances of getting hypoglycaemia.

Myth: Diabetics cannot participate in a Marathon

Fact: You can. Just ensure you consult your doctor for his professional advice, test your blood sugar before and after the race, it is also wise to carry snacks along.

Causes of Prediabetes

An organ called the pancreas is responsible for the production of a hormone called the insulin. When the insulin secreted by your body doesn't function as well as it is supposed to i.e. converting sugar in the body to energy, Prediabetes occurs. Insufficient insulin or insulin resistance is the primary cause of prediabetes.

Though the pancreas, in order to balance the blood sugar level, tries to keep up with the rising blood sugar level. It tries to produce more insulin to make the cells in the body respond to the conversion of sugar into energy. After being overworked, the pancreas fails to keep up with the increased production and blood sugar accumulates unhindered.

Risk Factors of Prediabetes

Glucose level accumulates in the blood when the insulin in your body is silent, this accumulation over time becomes harmful to the body. As discussed under the myths associated with Prediabetes, there are certain risk factors that makes one more likely to have prediabetes. They are as follows:

- Your racial background; African-American/black, Hispanic/Latino, Pacific Islander, Asian-American and Amerindians.

- Your weight: Overweight or Obese. Especially those with inflated bellies.
- Being genetically or biologically connected to a diabetic (type 2 diabetes) i.e. your father, mother, siblings etc.
- You had gestational diabetes (during pregnancy) or you gave birth to a baby that outweighed nine pounds.
- Your blood pressure level is spiking the charts (140/90 mm Hg).
- You have very low HDL cholesterol that is below 40mg per dL for males and 50mg per

dL for females or a triglyceride level that exceeds 250mg per dL.
- If you are a female diagnosed with Polycystic Ovary Syndrome (POCS).
- Living a sedentary lifestyle, that is a life devoid of regular physical activities to keep you fit.
- You are 45 years and above.
- Your waistline: having a waistline above 40 inches (for males) and 35 inches (for females) puts you at risk of being prediabetic.
- Regular consumption of red meat and processed foods, seldom or rarely eat whole foods, fruits and vegetables.

- Have or had a cardiovascular disease.
- Have other health issues as a result of insulin resistance.
- Smoking.
- Poor sleeping habits.

Ways to Fight, Prevent and Reverse Prediabetes

Fortunately, prediabetes is not some hard-core, incurable condition. As stated earlier, prediabetes can be prevented or reversed with changes in lifestyle. You should pay attention to certain things to be able to fight and reverse prediabetes. This is not only beneficial to prediabetics but also to everyone that considers their health important. These include:

Weight Loss

If your weight cannot be considered healthy and your waistline is evidently showing signs of fat accumulation, then you need to lose some of that weight. Weight gain automatically increases your blood pressure and cholesterol level and weight loss decreases them and keeps them at a healthy level.

Losing about seven percent of your weight is a good start to reversing prediabetes or preventing it. You don't need to shed all the fat on your body to be free from prediabetes.

Physical Fitness

Regular exercise is important and should be implemented with immediate effect. If you were lax in this aspect, it is time to up your fitness game. You don't necessarily have to be a regular face at the gym to keep fit. Carrying out physical activities is what's essential. Take brisk walks, swim, jog or cycle for about five times a week. Allocating at least thirty minutes of your time each day to carry out these physical activities, keeps you on track to prevent and reverse prediabetes.

Also, in the aspect of walking, walk more even when there are more convenient ways of doing a particular thing. For instance, use the stairs as an alternative to the elevator, instead of asking your meal to be delivered to you, walk to go get it, while taking public transport, come down some distance from your actual stop so you can walk the rest of the distance, arrange for walking breaks during meetings you attend as you tend to sit throughout such meeting, get a friend or colleague that will motivate you to stick to this plan.

The essence of this is that as you exert your body in carrying out physical activities, your muscle uses up the excess sugar in your blood by converting it to energy.

Dieting

Religiously follow a healthy meal plan, consume healthy foods e.g. vegetables, whole grains, lean protein, low-fat dairy and of course, fruits. Drink water instead of drinks packed with processed sugar.

Avoid excess intake of carbohydrates in your diet as it is the category of food that raises the level of blood sugar the most, causing the pancreas to work beyond its normal rate in producing insulin. Foods such as cake, rice, processed fruit juice, ice cream and so on are in this category.

Always go for whole instead of processed and canned foods. Ingesting whole milk is way better and healthier than processed and sweetened milk. Use honey instead of processed sugar to sweeten your foods.

Also avoid fried foods, they are a fast lane to high cholesterol level. In another chapter, I will discuss healthy recipes to follow and how to set up a meal plan.

The rate at which technology is advancing these days should make managing our health much easier. With your mobile phone or personal computer, and an internet connection, you get access to health resources and apps online that can help you plan a healthy diet, aid and guide you while you exercise and monitor your calories.

However, there are few cases of prediabetics where activities did not help to reverse the prediabetes neither did it lower their blood sugar level. The best solution in this case is medication. The most used medication for reducing blood sugar level and taming insulin resistance is **metformin**, commonly known as Glucophage. It is actually a drug for type 2 diabetics.

Unfortunately, metformin, like most drugs have side effects. The common ones include; bloating, diarrhoea, pain in the stomach region, indigestion, gas, heartburn, metallic taste etc.

Foods to Limit When Treating/ Preventing Prediabetic

- Vegetables rich in starch such as corn, sweet potatoes.
- Dried fruit and fruit juice.

- Beans, lentils and peas (Keto diet)
- Grains such as pretzels, white rice, white bread, white pasta etc.
- Yogurts with sweetened with artificial sweeteners.
- Synthetic foods such as tortilla chips, potato chips etc.
- Fried foods such as fried chicken, fried meat and French fries.
- Ice cream, pastries, pie, candy, cake and other sweet foods.
- Carbonated drinks, sweetened coffee, energy drinks etc.

Health Implications of Prediabetes

Health Implications refers to the several consequences that the body will suffer if Prediabetes is left unchecked and neglected. When sugar accumulates in the blood unhindered, it develops into type 2 diabetes.

This is more serious than prediabetes, it also involves huge amount of funds to manage and control. If type 2 diabetes is also left to worsen, and no form of treatment or anything is done about it, multiple organs in the body will likely get damaged. Vital organs being impaired opens up the body to further ailments, and this quickly cuts short the lifespan of the individual affected.

So, below are the varieties of complications that can arise from the neglect of prediabetes and ultimately, type 2 diabetes:

Cardiovascular Malfunction

"Cardiovascular" refers to the heart and the body's blood vessels. When prediabetes develops into type 2 diabetes, it significantly increases your chances of having heart disease, stroke, peripheral artery disease, and atherosclerosis.

Nerve Impairment

Not tending to your increasing blood sugar level over a period of time will likely result in the impairment of the nerves in your body. When that happens, it means you have "diabetic neuropathy".

You will experience insensitivity or loss of feeling in your upper and lower limbs (arms, fingers, toes and feet), you will also experience a painful sensation that begins from the end of your fingers, toes and moves up.

Other symptoms of this condition include throwing up, diarrhoea, lack of sex drive and issues in functioning sexually, indigestion, drowsiness and so on.

Issues with Eyesight

As said earlier, increasing blood sugar is capable of destroying the blood vessels that lead to the retina of the eyes. This could result in blindness. Other possible outcomes of this condition are contracting glaucoma or cataracts.

Kidney Damage

Over a period of time, an untreated diabetic condition affects the kidneys and they no longer filter blood as they should. This is a very serious complication as the impairment of the kidney will need to be treated with very expensive medical solutions such as a kidney transplant or dialysis.

Feet Damage

This condition is a consequence of diabetic neuropathy and impairment of the blood vessels. Trivial injuries such as surface wounds and blisters can escalate into ulcers, infections and amputation of the foot in a worst-case scenario. This is because the blood vessel connected to the feet is impaired and the wound fails to heal.

Skin and Oral Infections

Your chances of getting skin diseases, sores in the mouth and disease of the gum is much higher, with the unchecked increase of sugar in the blood over time.

Alzheimer's Disease

This disease is a very serious condition as it involves the brain cells. They get damaged due to their inability to access the energy they need from the glucose in the blood.

So, a diabetic who is doing nothing or very little in controlling his blood sugar increases his or her risk of contracting this deadly disease after some years.

Unlike the myths associated with Prediabetes and Diabetes which made the above-mentioned conditions seem inevitable and certain, it is certain that a poor lifestyle, the wrong diet and wrong medication can lead to complications.

A diabetic who takes the necessary steps to manage his blood sugar through changes in lifestyle, diet and proper medications, will definitely lower the risk of getting these complications because his blood sugar is kept in check and doesn't increase steadily.

Chapter Two

Explaining Diabetes

This is a plural condition actually because Diabetes is of varying types. They all have issues with one thing in common; the pancreatic hormone, insulin.

Issues such as the inability of the body to produce insulin, the body not producing sufficient amount of insulin and the body not responding as it should to the effect of insulin.

The body is literally made up of millions of cells that need glucose to function. That is their fuel. The stomach is responsible for breaking down much of the food we eat into glucose, which is then transported through the blood vessels to the various cells in the body. These cells draw energy from the glucose to use our day to day routine.

Insulin is the hormone in charge of regulating the amount of glucose in the bloodstream, it is secreted by the pancreas in small quantities. It works by entering the bloodstream from the pancreas and making sure that the glucose gets to the cells.

The more glucose builds up in the bloodstream, the more insulin is secreted by the pancreas, causing the sugar level to reduce. This leads to a balance in the blood sugar level, keeping it at a healthy range.

However, you need to eat regularly as staying hungry will cause your blood sugar level to drop drastically, leading to low blood sugar (hypoglycaemia). This is because the body cells will have to depend on the reserve glucose in your body for energy.

Now, diabetics have little or no insulin in their body to regulate their blood glucose level. In other cases, they actually have insulin but their body cells don't respond well to them. So, the blood sugar in their blood vessels keeps accumulating till it gets high enough to be harmful to health. This disease is diagnosed the exact same way Prediabetes is tested for.

Type of Diabetes

Type 1 Diabetes

Also called juvenile diabetes and insulin-dependent diabetes. It is a chronic condition.

This occurs when the beta cells i.e. the cells responsible for the secretion of insulin in the body, have been impaired by the immune system.

As a result, the body is incapable of producing insulin and then needs insulin therapy to control the blood glucose level.

It can affect individuals at any age but it is common among children and teenagers. Type 1 Diabetes has no cure yet. It can only be managed and treated via medications such as insulin injections, a healthy diet and lifestyle so as to prevent complications.

Symptoms of Type 1 Diabetes

- Intensified thirst.
- Increased rate of urination.
- Intense hunger.
- Bed-wetting starts becoming a part of children who usually do not bed-wet before.
- Mood swings and irritation.
- Involuntary weight loss.
- Exhaustion and lack of strength.
- Blurry eyesight.

Causes of Type 1 Diabetes

- The insulin-producing cells is destroyed by the immune system.
- Genetic trait.
- Environmental exposure.
- Viruses.

Known risk factors associated with this type of diabetes includes: genes, environmental location, age (mostly during prepubescence and adolescence), family tree.

Complications associated with the type 1 diabetes are identical to those associated with type 2 diabetes.

Type 2 Diabetes

It is also referred to as Diabetes mellitus type 2, *adult-onset diabetes*, or noninsulin-dependent diabetes mellitus. Type 2 diabetics produce insulin in their body, but It is a case of the insulin being insufficient or not being identified and utilized adequately, resulting in the accumulation of blood sugar in the body.

This is the most popular form of diabetes and though prevention is very much possible for this, it is at the forefront of diabetes-induced complications such as blindness, neuropathy, limb amputations, dialysis etc.

Insulin resistance occurs when the body cells is unable to respond to the normal levels of insulin, precisely within the muscle, fat and liver tissue. The liver is a storeroom for blood glucose as well. It is the insulin that keeps the glucose in the liver in check. In a case where the insulin is deficient in the body, the liver indiscriminately releases glucose into the bloodstream. Not all cases of insulin resistance results in type 2 diabetes because for type 2 diabetes to happen, the insulin secretion by the pancreas needs to be impaired as well.

According to Wikipedia, type 2 diabetes makes up for an overwhelming 90% of all diabetic cases, while the remaining 10% is shared between type 1 diabetes and gestational diabetes.

Obesity and sedentary lifestyle are the primary causes of type 2 diabetes, though there are cases of people with healthy weights being diabetic, but a vast majority are overweight people.

According to Wikipedia, since 1960, the frequency of type 2 diabetes has steadily risen in concordance with obesity. In 1985, 38 million people were suffering from type 2 diabetes, this figure increased astronomically several years later. In 2015, the figure was at 392 million people around the globe.

Though the disease most commonly occurs during middle age and above, it is now occurring more often in younger people. This is partially because of the complications that results from type 2 diabetes when left untreated.

The symptoms and causes of this type of diabetes is identical to that of prediabetes since type 2 diabetes is what Prediabetes develops into if not treated and prevented.

Thiazides, Statins, Glucocorticoids, beta blockers and atypical antipsychotics are some of the medications that can make individuals vulnerable to type 2 diabetes.

Health issues such as gestational diabetes, acromegaly, Cushing's syndrome, hyperthyroidism, certain cancers and deficiency in testosterone levels also make individuals vulnerable to type 2 diabetes.

While type 2 diabetes is described by insulin resistance and partial insulin deficiency, type 1 diabetes is a case of total insulin deficiency.

In any case, the diagnosis doesn't clearly distinguish whether it is type 1 or 2, antibody diagnosis will identify for type 1 and C-peptide levels identify for type 2 diabetes.

Type 2 diabetes can be prevented the same way Prediabetes is prevented. This is because preventing prediabetes also prevents type 2 diabetes. Change in lifestyle is a better way of handling diabetes than taking Metformin. This is because over time, change in lifestyle lowers the risk of type 2 diabetes by about 28% unlike medications that does not lower the risk after withdrawal from such medications.

Surgery undergone by overweight people to lose weight is a powerful way to treat diabetes. This helps them maintain a healthy blood sugar level with the aid of no medication or medication taken in very little quantities. This treatment is best for people who haven't been able to get their blood sugar and weight in check despite changes in diet and exercises.

Gestational Diabetes

It is also called *Gestational Diabetes Mellitus*. This is a condition in which a non-diabetic female develops an unhealthy level of blood sugar during her trimesters of pregnancy. It usually starts during the last trimester of the pregnancy. This condition shoots up the risk of depression, pre-eclampsia and it may need Caesarean section.

Foetus being formed during a pregnancy associated with gestational diabetes may develop jaundice and low blood sugar, if the condition of the mother is not treated properly. It can also be the cause of stillbirth. In the long run, it can result in the child developing type 2 diabetes and becoming obese.

This condition is caused by insulin resistance in the body. Like other forms of diabetes, diagnosis is by blood test. Certain risk factors are involved as well.

Factors such as; past experience with gestational diabetes, belonging to a family with a history of type 2 diabetes, polycystic ovarian syndrome and obesity.

For expecting mothers at relative risk, screening for this is best done between 24-28 weeks of gestation. For those at a greater risk, screening is best done at the first prenatal trip.

You can prevent gestational diabetes by making sure your weight is at a healthy level and proper fitness activities before you get pregnant.

To treat gestational diabetes, one would need dieting, fitness activities and maybe insulin injections. It may not get to receiving insulin shots as regular exercise and dieting helps women check their blood sugar level. It is advisable for the gestational diabetics to test their blood sugar about four times a day. This condition affects an estimate of 3-9% of pregnancies. In most cases of gestational diabetes, the condition disappears after childbirth but the woman is at increased risk of contracting type 2 diabetes.

Gestational Diabetics are females who may either have had diabetes undetected in their body or they became diabetic in a coincidental event with the pregnancy. A woman becomes a gestational diabetic when glucose intolerance surpasses 24-28 weeks of pregnancy.

Chapter Three

Setting up a Diet Plan

Eating healthy is extremely essential to reversing prediabetes or managing diabetes. With a good diet plan, one can maintain his blood glucose level, and significantly lower his or her chances of facing the complications that comes with the stay of an untreated diabetes over a period of time.

Diet plans comes in various categories or styles, a diabetic-diet features more of foods rich in fiber, lean proteins and healthy fats and puts a limit to the intake of carbohydrates such as white bread, rice etc.

Just as people are different, so are their needs and preferences. A certain meal plan that appeals to a certain diabetic may not appeal to others, so dieting has to be flexible so it can be planned according to the particular individual's preferences. There is nothing like a general meal plan for all diabetic patients.

A meal plan has various durations depending on the preference of the individual. It could be very short term, relatively short term or medium term. It could be for as little as 3 days to as much as a month.

A meal plan designed to manage and reverse prediabetes needs to tick the following criteria:

- Include foods you like and enjoy eating.
- Allow you indulge yourself and get satisfaction from your cravings at events and other occasions.
- They should be foods you can easily find to purchase.
- Are not time consuming to prepare.

Types of Diet

Keto Diet

This is the perfect diet for those seeking to shed some weight especially if they are obese. It is a diet that gives room for flexibility; which is one of the key qualities to a good diet. It makes some kind of room or allowances and it can adjust to certain preferences. The diet is essentially about low amount of carbohydrates, more of whole grains but then certain preferences like adjusting one's intake of carbohydrates can be done as long as the intake doesn't go overboard.

While some might include very little carbohydrates, others might up its quantity a bit as long as it is smaller than the whole grains in the diet.

Carbohydrates such as artificially preserved and processed foods, starch and sugars comes in minute quantities.

tables, fruits, eggs, lean meat, nuts, fish and healthy fats, make up the bulk of the diet.

Mediterranean Diet

This is a very good diet. It is very good in preventing one from developing cardiovascular diseases. The diet derives its name from its content. Its content focuses on meals that were eaten during and before the twentieth century in the Mediterranean territories.

It includes plenty of poultry, vegetables, fish, whole grains, legumes, dairy products and of course, Olive oil.

Paleo Diet

This diet is recommended for losing weight and improving health. It is currently the most recognised diet globally. It centres on whole foods that is identical to the ones consumed by some of the earliest generations on earth.

Vegan Diet

This particular diet has been enjoying increasing recognition of recent; for the past ten years or thereabouts. This diet is associated to improvement in cardiovascular health, an effective regulation of blood sugar and loss of weight.

Its content includes fruits and vegetables and that's about it.

Anti-Gluten/Gluten-Free Diet

This diet is recommended for people with gluten intolerance. Gluten is a protein that is present in barley, wheat and rye.

It contains foods that are free from gluten, precisely whole foods.

Snacks that can Regulate your Blood Glucose Level

It is possible to stick to healthy meal plans and yet not achieve the goal of stabilizing your blood sugar level. Adding healthy snacks to your food intake for the day can help a long way in achieving this goal.

Improved eating routine doesn't mean you should eat less. Rather, it means you should consume more quality foods. Going several hours without food only makes it harder to regulate your blood sugar level, doing this consistently may cause low blood sugar. You may also tend to overeat when next you see food. There should be evenly paced intervals between meals and snacks should come in between at some point.

Eating snacks helps to prevent you from eating excessively at the next meal time, it also prevents the highs and lows of your blood sugar level that may result from

...nt eating, fasting and...

Healthy snacks should be taken, not just any snack as most snacks are junk and they have little or no nutritional value.

Hummus and Veggies

Hummus is a finished product from olive oil, chickpeas, and tahini (sesame seed paste). It is rich in protein, complex carbohydrates and fats that are good for the heart. This Mediterranean delicacy combines perfectly with vegetables that are rich in fiber. Examples include; cucumbers, celery or carrots etc.

Fruits and Greek Yogurt

These are both sweet foods but yet for some reason, they are also friendly to your blood glucose level. It is recommended for those prediabetics or diabetics with sweet tooth.

Greek yogurt was prepared using a peculiar straining process so it has rich proteins and healthy bacteria unlike other varieties of yogurts.

Most yogurts have sweeteners or syrups added to them, making them junk yogurt. The best bet is to go for your plain Yogurt and take it together with a tasty, fresh fruit.

Nut Butter and Apple

The best way to consume an apple is with the skin. Never peel off the skin when eating an apple, it is a great source of fiber. Having an apple to go with your favourite nut butter is a combination for a healthy, energy-giving snack.

Ensure your nut butter is free from added sweeteners or unhealthy oils. Whether it is peanut butter, almond butter or cashew butter, a healthy nut butter is going to be made up of just the nut paste and salt.

Whole Grain Crackers and Tuna Fish

Tuna fish is an enormous source of protein and it is considered a super food because it also contains omega-3 fatty acids, which according to some research on it, can lessen inflammation in the body and boost the sensitivity of insulin.

Combining this superfood with a high-fiber, whole grain cracker gives your body access to complex carbohydrates, super protein and healthy fats.

Setting up a Meal Plan

This is a recommended meal plan for a 7-day period. This meal plan consists of meals and snacks that make up some of the best food for a diabetic condition. It is a rich arrangement and combination of lean proteins, healthy fats, fruits, veggies and whole grains into different intervals of the day.

Processed carbohydrates such as white rice, bread and pasta are limited here. Also limited is sodium and saturated fats. Each meal has a carb serving of about 30-45grams while each snack has a serving of 15grams of carbohydrates.

A 7-Day 1,200 Calories (per day) Meal Plan.

Day 1

Breakfast: Oats served with Walnut and Plum.

(41 grams of carbs and 294 calories).

Morning Snack: Greek Yogurt and Blueberries.

(96 calories and 18 grams of carbs).

Lunch: Apple Cheddar Melt and Turkey

(319 calories and 37 grams of carbs).

Afternoon Snack: Apple, Honey and Cinnamon.

(58 calories and 16 grams of carbs).

Dinner: Rosemary-Goat Cheese Toast and Vegetable Soup

(417 calories and 54 grams of carbs).

Day 2

Breakfast: Avocado Toast, Blueberries and Pistachios.

(297 calories and 33 grams of carbs).

Morning Snack: Cherries

(52 calories and 13 grams of carbs).

Lunch: Wheat Baguette with Vegetable Soup

(314 calories and 47 grams of carbs).

Afternoon Snack: Apples and Cinnamon

(95 calories and 25 grams of carbs).

Dinner: Lentil and Roasted Vegetable Salad with Green Goddess Dressing.

(429 calories and 48 grams of carbs).

Day 3

Breakfast: Yogurt, Flaxseed and Walnuts

(289 calories and 27 grams of carbs).

Morning Snack: Plum

(30 calories and 8 grams of carbs).

Lunch: Apple Slices and Lentils with Mixed Greens

(347 calories and 48 grams of carbs)

Afternoon Snack: Oranges

(Contains 62 calories and 15 grams of carbs)

Dinner: Rice, Chicken Sausage & Peppers with Vegetable Salad

(Contains 490 calories and 52 grams of carbs)

Day 4

Breakfast: Oatmeal, Flaxseed, Plum and Walnuts.

This is a repeat of Day 1 breakfast with the addition of the flaxseed.

(Contains 295 calories and 42 grams of carbs)

Morning Snack: 10 Cherries

(Contains 52 calories and 13 grams of carbs).

Lunch: Dried Apricots with Veggie and Hummus Sandwich.

Eat a single serving of the sandwich with three dried apricots.

(Contains 350 calories and 46 grams of sandwich).

Afternoon Snack: Orange

(Contains 62 calories and 15 grams of carbs).

One medium-sized orange.

Dinner: Lemon-Herb Salmon with Caponata and Farro.

A single serving of Lemon-Herb salmon with Caponata and Farro or other any whole grain such as brown rice.

(Contains 450 calories and 46 grams of carbs)

Day 5

Breakfast: Bagel Avocado Toast and Cherries.

A single serving of the Bagel Avocado Toast to go with 20 cherries.

(Contains 276 calories and 44 grams of carbs)

Morning Snack: Dried Apricots.

(Contains 51 calories and 13 grams of carbs)

Lunch: Turkey with Pear Pita Melt & Plum.

(Contains 350 calories and 41 grams of carbs).

Afternoon Snack: Cinnamon & Pear.

Slice a medium-sized pear into halve, chop and serve with cinnamon to taste.

(Contains 52 calories and 15 grams of carbs).

Dinner: Spaghetti Squash & Meatballs, Toasted Baguette with Goat Cheese.

A single serving of Spaghetti Squash & meatballs, a quarter-inch thick slice of

Baguette, ½ spoon of goat cheese and ¼ spoon of freshly sliced rosemary.

(Contains 448 calories and 38 grams of carbs)

Day 6

Breakfast: Yogurt, Flaxseed and Walnuts.

(291 calories, 28 grams of carbs).

One serving of yogurt and blueberries with honey, 2 spoons of grinded flaxseed and walnuts.

Morning Snack: 14 Cherries

(18 grams of carbs, 72 calories).

Lunch: Vegetable Soup

(42 grams of carbs, 337 calories).

Serve two and half cups of vegetable soup for lunch.

Afternoon Snack: One medium-sized Orange

(15 grams of carbs, 62 calories).

Dinner: Apple-glazed Chicken with Spinach & Steamed Butternut Squash.

(422 calories, 53 grams of carbs).

Day 7

Breakfast: Blueberries Pecan Pancakes with Flaxseed.

(300 calories and 40 grams of carbs).

Morning Snack: Orange

(62 calories, 15 grams of carbs).

Lunch: Vegetable Salad with Mixed Greens, Toasted Pita and Hummus.

(325 calories and 35 grams of carbs).

Afternoon Snack: Apple

(95 calories and 25 grams of carbs).

Dinner: Mushroom-Sauced Pork Chops, Brown Rice and Roasted Brussels Sprouts with Sun-Dried Tomato Pesto.

(444 calories and 48 grams)

Chapter Four

Prediabetes Friendly Recipes

Coconut Shrimps

Total Duration: 10-15 mins.

Ingredients

- Sweetened coconuts – ¼ cup.
- Cup of panko breadcrumbs – ¼ cup.
- Kosher salt – ½ tablespoon.
- Coconut milk – ½ cup.
- Shrimps, deveined and peeled – 12.

Instructions

- Heat the oven to 375 F. Sparingly coat the baking sheet with cooking spray.

- Process the coconut, Salt and Panko inside a food processor till the consistency of the mixture is even.
- Pour the mixture into a small bowl. Also pour the coconut milk into another bowl.
- Douse each shrimp into the panko mixture first, then the coconut milk next, and place it on top of the baking sheet.
- Pour a little cooking spray on the shrimp to give it a thin coating.
- Heat in the oven till it's golden brown in colour, for about ten to fifteen minutes.

Nutritional Value

Serving Size: 2 shrimps.

Calories: 75g   Monounsaturated fat: 2g

Total fat: 4g   Total sugars: 2g

Saturated fat: 2g   Sodium: 396mg

Cholesterol: 48mg   Total carbs: 4g

Protein: 5g

Black Bean and Corn Relish.

Total Duration: 31-32 mins.

Ingredients

- Black beans, rinsed and drained – 2 cups or 15.5 ounces.

- Frozen corn kernels, defrosted to room temperature – 1 cup.
- Tomatoes, seeded and diced – 3 cups.
- Garlic cloves, chopped – 2
- Medium-sized red onion, chopped – ½ cup.
- Chopped parsley – ½ cup.
- Bell pepper (red, yellow or green) – 1.
- Lemon Juice extract – 1 lemon.
- Sugar – 2 teaspoons.

Instructions

- Combine all the ingredients in a large mixing bowl.
- Mix by gently tossing the bowl.

- Cover and place in the refrigerator for about 30 minutes to allow the flavours blend properly.
- Serve after the time allocated in the previous step.

Nutritional Value

Serving Size: 1 cup

Calories: 112   Dietary Fiber: 6g

Total Fat: 0.5g   Total Carbs: 22g

Protein: 5g   Added Sugars: 1g

Saturated Fat: Trace   Sodium: 93mg

Total Sugars: 3g

Monounsaturated Fat: Trace

Fruit Salsa and Tortilla Chips

Cooking Duration: 10-12 mins (for the Tortilla chips)

Ingredients

For Tortilla Crisps

- Whole wheat fat-free tortilla – 8.
- Sugar – 1 tablespoon.
- Cinnamon – ½ tablespoon.
- Cooking Spray

For Fruit Salsa

- Diced pieces of fresh fruits (apples, grapes, berries, orange and so on) – 3 cups.
- Any flavour of sugar-free jam – 2 tablespoons.

- Honey or agave nectar – 1 tablespoon.
- Orange Juice – 2 tablespoons.

Instructions

- Preheat the oven to 350 F, then divide each tortilla into 8 wedges.
- Place them on two baking sheets, not touching each other. Coat them with cooking spray.
- Mix sugar and cinnamon in a small mixing bowl, then spray the mixture on the tortillas.
- Bake the pieces till they are crisp. This should take between 10-12 minutes.

- Transfer the tortillas to a rack to cool.
- Chop the fruit into cubes, then gently combine them in a bowl.
- Take another bowl, whisk jam, honey and orange juice together and pour the mixture on the fruits. Then mix gently.
- Use plastic wrap to cover the bowl and refrigerate for about 2 to 3 hours (this should be done ahead of the appetizer)
- Serve as a dip for the tortilla chips.

Nutritional Value

Serving size: 1/3 cup of Salsa, 8 Chips.

Total Carbs: 24g   Trans Fat: Trace

Calories: 105   Dietary Fiber: 10g

Sodium: 181mg   Saturated Fat: Trace

Total Fat: Trace   Protein: 2g

Total Sugars: 8g   Added Sugars: 4g

Monounsaturated Fat: Trace

Artichoke Dip

Cooking Duration: 30 mins.

Ingredients

- Artichoke hearts in water, drained – 1 can (15.5oz).
- Minced garlic – 2 cloves.
- Chopped Fresh Spinach – 4 cups.

- Minced fresh thyme – 1 teaspoon.
- Ground black pepper – 1 teaspoon.
- Fresh minced parsley – 1 tablespoon.
- Cooked unsalted white beans – 1 cup.
- Grated Parmesan Cheese – 2 tablespoons.
- Low-fat sour cream – half cup.

Instructions

- Mix all the ingredients in a mixing bowl.
- Put the mixture in a ceramic plate and heat it on 350F for 30 mins. Serve warm.

Nutritional Value

Serving Size - half a cup.

Total Carbs: 10g   Total Sugars: 1.5g

Dietary Fiber: 6g   Protein: 5g

Saturated Fat: 1g   Sodium: 130mg

Monounsaturated Fat: Trace

Total Fat: 2g   Calories: 78

Cholesterol: 6mg

Artichokes Alla Romana

Cooking Duration: 60-70 mins.

Ingredients

- Whole wheat bread crumbs – 2 cups.

- Olive oil – 1 tablespoon.
- Large globe artichokes – 4.
- Grated parmesan cheese – 1/3 cup.
- Lemon halves – 2.
- Garlic cloves, finely chopped – 3.
- Fresh flat parsley, finely chopped – 2 tablespoons.
- Grated lemon zest – 1 tablespoon.
- Freshly ground black pepper – ¼ cup.
- Low-sodium vegetable or chicken-stock – 1 cup plus 2-4 tablespoons.
- Dry white wine – 1 cup.
- Minced shallot – 1 tablespoon.

- Fresh oregano, chopped – 1 teaspoon.

Instructions

- Heat the oven to 400 F. Use a bowl to mix the breadcrumbs and olive oil.
- Toss to coat. Use a shallow baking pan to spread the crumbs and bake. Stir once halfway till the crumbs are a bit golden. This should take about 10 minutes.
- Taking one artichoke at a time, pluck out any tough outer leaves, cut the stem flush with the base.
- Use a serrated knife to cut off the third top of the leaves. Also

cut the remaining thorns with scissors.
- Use a lemon half to rub the edges of the stem to prevent discolouration. Pull out the small leaves from the centre and separate the inner leaves.
- Use a spoon to scoop out the fuzzy choke and squeeze some lemon juice into the cavity. Repeat the process with the other artichokes.
- Use a large bowl to combine the breadcrumbs, parmesan, parsley, garlic, lemon zest and pepper. Add 2-4 tablespoons of vegetable or chicken stock, ensure you put in one spoon at a time, just put in

enough to make the combination in the bowl to start developing clumps.
- Take 2/3 of the mixture and mound it in the center of the artichoke.
- Start spreading the leaves from the bottom, applying a full teaspoon near the base of each of the open leaves (This should be done ahead of time and kept in the refrigerator).
- Use a Dutch oven with a tight-fitting lid, combine the white wine, shallot, oregano and the remaining one cup of stock.
- Once it starts boiling, reduce the heat to low heat.

- Arrange the artichokes in the liquid in a single layer, stem-down. Cover the lid and let it simmer for about 45 minutes (if necessary, add more water).
- Remove the artichokes and place them on a rack to cool. Once warm, cut into quarters and serve.

Nutritional Value

Serving Size: ¼ artichoke

Saturated Fat: 1g   Monounsaturated Fat: 2g

Trans Fat: Trace   Total Fat: 3g

Calories: 123   Cholesterol: 3mg

Sodium: 179mg   Total Sugars: 2g

Total Carbs: 18g   Dietary Fiber: 5g

Protein: 6g

Buckwheat Pancakes with Strawberry Toppings

Cooking Duration: 7-8 mins.

Ingredients

- Canola Oil – 1 tablespoon.
- Egg whites – 2.
- All-purpose flour – ½ cup.
- Fat-free milk – ½ cup.
- Buckwheat flour – ½ cup.
- Baking powder – 1 tablespoon.
- Sugar – 1 tablespoon.
- Sparkling water – ½ cup.

- Strawberries, freshly sliced – 3 cups.

Instructions

- Mix the egg whites, milk and canola oil in a bowl.
- Mix the flour, sugar and baking powder in a separate bowl.
- Pour the mixture in the first bowl into the second bowl, and turn till it's a smooth, slightly moist batter.
- Place a pan or griddle over medium heat.
- Test the temperature of the pan with a drop of water, if the water sizzles on contact, the pan is ready for the pancakes.

- Spoon a half cup of the pancake batter into the pan.
- Cook until the top surface bubbles and the edges of the pancake is light brown. This will take about 2 minutes.
- Turn over the pancake and cook till the bottom is very brown. This will take about 2 minutes.
- Repeat the same process with the other pancakes.
- Serve the pancakes warm on a plate and top a half cup of strawberries on each pancake.

Nutritional Value

Serving size: 2 small Pancakes.

Calories: 143   Total Sugars: 6.5g

Saturated Fat: Trace   Total Fat: 3g

Monounsaturated Fat: 2g

Cholesterol: Trace Dietary Fiber: 3g

Sodium: 150mg   Protein: 5g

Total Carbs: 24g   Added Sugars: 2g

Ham, Pineapple and Asparagus Crepes.

Cooking Duration: 7-9 mins.

Ingredients

- Asparagus Stalks – 6 halves.
- Pre-packaged crepes – 4.
- Reduced-sodium, extra-lean ham, thinly sliced – 8 ounces.

- Crushed pineapples, drained of juice – half cup.
- Shredded reduced-fat Co-Jack cheese – half cup.

Instructions

- Preheat the oven to 350 F. Sparingly coat the baking dish with cooking spray.
- Put 1 inch of water into a pot with steamer basket, put in the asparagus, cover and steam till it's tender and crisp. This will take at least 2 minutes.
- Put the crepes into the microwave to heat for about a minute.

- Put 2 ounces of ham, three Asparagus Stalks, 2 tablespoons of cheese and 2 tablespoons of crushed pineapples on each crepe.
- Roll the crepe up and place on its side in the preheated baking dish.
- Bake the crepe till the cheese melts. This will take about 3 minutes. Serve at once.

Nutritional Value

Serving Size: 1 crepe.

Calories: 253   Sodium: 742mg

Saturated Fat: 6g   Total Fat: 13g

Monounsaturated Fat: 4gTotal Sugars: 9g

Cholesterol: 127mg   Total Carbs: 21g

Dietary Fiber: 1g   Protein: 18g

Raspberry Chocolate Scones

Cooking Duration: 10-12 mins.

Ingredients

- Whole-wheat pastry flour – 1 cup.
- All-purpose flour – 1 cup.
- Baking Powder – 1 tablespoon.
- Baking soda – a quarter tablespoon.
- Fat-free butter spread – 1/3 cup.
- Fresh or frozen raspberries – half cup.
- Small chocolate chips – a quarter cup.
- Fat-free Yogurt – 1 cup + 2 tablespoons.

- Honey – 2 tablespoons.
- Sugar – half teaspoon.
- Cinnamon – quarter teaspoon

Instructions

- Use a large mixing bowl to mix the baking soda, baking powder and the flours.
- Cut in crumbly buttery spread, add chocolates chips and berries. Gently mix them.
- Mix honey and Yogurt together using a small mixing bowl.
- Add Yogurt mixture to flour mixture and mix till you get a smooth consistency.

- Knead the ball of dough one or two times, roll into a half-inch circle.
- Cut into twelve wedges and place on a thinly greased baking surface.
- Mix sugar and cinnamon using a small bowl, drizzle mixture on top of scones.
- Bake the scones at 400 F for about 10-12 minutes. Remove and let it cool before you serve.

Nutritional Value

Serving Size: 1 scone.

Calories: 149   Saturated Fat: 1.5g

Total Fat: 5g   Trans Fat: Trace

Monounsaturated Fat: 2g

Sodium: 143mg   Cholesterol: Trace

Total Carbs: 22g   Protein: 4g

Dietary Fiber: 2g   Added Sugars: 3g

Rhubarb Pecan Muffins

Cooking Duration: 30-35 mins.

Ingredients

- All-purpose flour – 1 cup.
- Whole wheat flour – 1 cup.
- Sugar – ½ cup.
- Baking Powder – 1 ½ teaspoon.
- Baking soda – ½ cup.
- Salt – ½ cup.
- Egg whites – 2.
- Canola oil – 2 tablespoons.

- Unsweetened apple sauce – 2 tablespoons.
- Grated orange peel – 2 teaspoons.
- Calcium-fortified orange juice – ¾ cup.
- Rhubarb, finely chopped – 1 ¼ cups.
- Chopped pecans – 2 tablespoons.

Instructions

- Preheat the oven to 350 F. Use foil liners to line your muffin pan.
- Use a large bowl to mix the baking powder, sugar, salt, baking soda and flour and stir till you get an even consistency.

- Use a separate bowl to mix the canola oil, egg whites, applesauce, orange juice and orange peel then put into an electric mixer to mix it till it's smooth.
- Add the flour mixture and continue mixing till it's moistened.
- Add the chopped rhubarb and mix.
- Use a spoon till scoop the batter into 12 muffin cups, with each cup being 2/3 full.
- Drizzle ½ teaspoon of chopped pecans onto each muffin, then bake it till it's rubbery to the

touch. This should take about 25-30 minutes.

- Put off the heat in the oven for it to cool for about 5 minutes, then place the muffins on the rack to complete the cooling process.

Nutritional Value

Serving Size: 1 muffin.

Calories: 143   Total Fat: 3g

Sodium: 190mg   Dietary Fiber: 2g

Total Carbs: 26g   Protein: 3g

Saturated Fat: 1g   Added Sugars: 8g

Trans Fat: Trace   Monounsaturated Fat: 2g

Muesli Breakfast Bars

Cooking Duration: about 60 mins.

Ingredients

- Old-fashioned rolled oats – 2 ½ cups.
- Soy Flour – ½ cup.
- Fat-free dry milk – ½ cup.
- Toasted wheat germ – ½ cup.
- Sliced almonds or chopped, toasted pecans – ½ cup.
- Dried, chopped apples – ½ cup.
- Raisins – ½ cup.
- Salt – ½ teaspoon.
- Dark honey – 1 cup.
- Natural unsalted peanut butter – ½ cup.
- Olive oil – 1 tablespoon.

- Vanilla extract – 2 teaspoons.

Instructions

- Preheat the oven to 350 F, use a 9 by 13-inch pan and coat the base with cooking spray.
- Mix the flour, almonds/ pecans, raisins, salt, dried milk, apples, oats, wheat germ in a large bowl. Mix gently and set aside.
- Use a small saucepan to mix the honey, peanut butter and salt over slightly low heat till you achieve a perfect blend.
- Stir in the vanilla, ensure your mixture doesn't boil. Reduce the heat if you have to.

- Add the warm mixture to the dry ingredients and stir till they are well combined. The paste should be sticky not wet.
- Place the paste with a spoon gently to even its spread on the baking pan and press the paste gently on the pan to remove any pockets.
- Bake till the edges starts getting brown. This should take about 25 minutes.
- Remove the pan from the oven and let it cool on a rack for about 10 minutes, then cut it into two dozen bars.
- If the bars are not yet cool enough, cool them directly on

the rack, package it into airtight containers and refrigerate till it solidifies well.

Nutritional Value

Serving Size: 1 bar

Total Carbs: 26g

Sodium: 81mg

Dietary Fiber: 2g

Total Fat: 5g

Calories: 169

Saturated Fat: 1g

Protein: 5g Monounsaturated Fat: 1g

Total Sugars: 17g

Added Sugars: 11g

Baked Macaroni with Red Sauce.

Cooking Duration: 45-50 mins.

Ingredients

- Extra-lean ground beef – ½ cup.
- Small onion, diced – ½ cup.
- Wheat elbow macaroni – 7 ounces.
- Low-sodium Spaghetti sauce – 1 jar.
- Parmesan Cheese – 6 tablespoons.

Instructions

- Preheat the oven to 350 F, use the cooking spray to thinly coat the baking dish.
- Use a frying pan to cook the onions and ground beef till the beef is browned and the onions is translucent. Remove and drain.

- Fill up ¾ of a large pot to boil, put the pasta and parboil. This should take 10-12 minutes, remove the pasta and drain completely.
- Mix the pasta and Spaghetti sauce with the beef and onions and stir well. Put the mixture on the baking dish, bake until it bubbles. This should take about 25-35 minutes.
- Share the macaroni into separate plates, top each plate with parmesan cheese then serve at once.

Nutritional Value

Serving size: About 1 cup.

Calories: 269   Sodium: 125mg

Cholesterol: 32mg Protein: 15g

Saturated Fat: 3g Total Fat: 9g

Trans Fat: Trace Total Carbs: 32g

Dietary Fiber: 4g Total Sugars: 6g

Monounsaturated Fat: 3g

Balsamic Feta Chicken

Cooking Duration: 35-40 mins.

Ingredients

- Chicken breasts – 6
- Balsamic vinegar – ½ cup
- Brown sugar – 2 tablespoons
- Olive oil – 1 tablespoon
- Paprika – 1 tablespoon

- Kosher salt – ½ teaspoon
- Fresh thyme, chopped – 1 teaspoon
- Dry mustard – ¼ tablespoon
- Crumbled feta cheese – 6 tablespoons

Instructions

- Preheat the oven to 350 F, lightly coat the baking dish with olive oil/cooking spray.
- Combine the brown sugar, chicken breasts, olive oil, paprika, vinegar, salt, thyme and mustard.
- Use tongs to coat the chicken, and let it marinate for a minimum of 20 minutes in the refrigerator.

- Remove the chicken breasts from the refrigerator and bake it on the baking sheets for about 15 minutes or till the temperature of the chicken reaches 165 F.
- Sprinkle cheese on each breast and serve.

Nutritional Value

Serving size: 1 breast.

Cholesterol: 79mg

Calories: 279

Total Fat: 15g

Sodium: 337mg

Total Sugars: 8g

Monounsaturated Fat: 6g

Saturated Fat: 4g

Total Carbs: 9g

Protein: 25g

Dietary Fiber: 1g

Barbecue Chicken Pizza

Cooking Duration: 15-17 mins.

Ingredients

- Salt-free tomato sauce – 1 cup
- 12-thin pizza crust – 1
- Tomato, sliced – 1
- Green pepper rings – 8
- Mushroom, sliced – 1 cup
- Cooked chicken breast, cut an inch thick with all visible fat layers removed – 4 ounces
- Barbecue sauce – 4 tablespoons
- Shredded mozzarella cheese with reduced fat – 1 cup

Instructions

- Preheat the oven to 400 F.

- Pour the sauce evenly on the pizza crust.
- Add the tomatoes, pepper, chicken and mushrooms.
- Then lightly pour the barbecue sauce on the pizza, then top it with the shredded cheese.
- Bake in the oven for at least 12 minutes. When done, divide into 8 slices and serve.

Nutritional Value

Serving size: 2 slices.

Calories: 384		Dietary Fiber: 4g

Total Carbs: 48g	Saturated Fat: 4g

Sodium: 749mg	Cholesterol: 39mg

Protein: 21mg		Total Fat: 12g

Monounsaturated Fat: 1.5g

Beef with Vegetable Stew

Cooking Duration: About 80 mins.

Ingredients

- Canola Oil – 2 teaspoons.
- Beef round steak – 1 pound.
- Chopped yellow onions – 2 cups.
- Chopped Celery – 1 cup.
- Chopped Roma tomatoes – 1 cup.
- Chopped sweet potato – ½ cup.
- Chopped white potato with skin – ½ cup.
- Chopped mushrooms – ½ cup.
- Chopped garlic- 4 cloves

- Chopped carrot – 1 cup.
- Chopped Kale – 1 cup.
- Fresh Barley – ¼ cup.
- Balsamic vinegar - 1 teaspoon.
- Minced fresh thyme – 1 teaspoon
- Red wine vinegar – ¼ cup.
- Dried, minced rosemary – 1 teaspoon.
- Low-sodium beef stock – 3 cups.
- Dried sage, crushed – 1 teaspoon
- Dried oregano – 1 tablespoon.
- Minced fresh parsley – 1 tablespoon
- Black pepper (to taste)

Instructions

- Turn on the heat on your broiler or grill. Set it to medium.

- Trim the gristle and fat on your steak.
- Grill the steak till it's brown, turning over only once. This should take not more than 14 minutes to avoid it getting overcooked.
- Remove from the grill and let it cool while you prepare the vegetables.
- Sauté vegetables in oil in a large stock pot till it's brown. This will take about 10 minutes. Add barley and let the vegetables cook for 5 more minutes.
- Use paper towels to pat-dry the steak, then add them to the pot after cutting them into half-inch

pieces. Add spices, herbs and vinegar.
- Let it boil and simmer for 1 hour till the stew is relatively thick and the barley is cooked.
- Serve hot.

Nutritional Value

Serving size: about two cups

Sodium: 138mg	Calories: 216
Protein: 21g	Cholesterol: 46mg
Saturated Fat: 1g	Total Carbs: 24g
Trans Fat: Trace	Total Fat: 4g
Total sugars: 7g	Monounsaturated Fat: 2g

Italian Meatballs

Cooking Duration: 20-25 mins.

Ingredients

- Large onion, minced – 1/3 cup.
- Minced garlic – 2½ teaspoons.
- Kosher salt – 1 teaspoon
- Grated parmesan cheese – 6 tablespoons
- Chopped Flats leaf-Italian parsley – 1/3 cup
- Egg whites – 1½ tablespoons
- Lean ground beef – 1½ Pounds
- Ground black pepper – 1/8 teaspoon

Instructions

- Heat the oven to 350 F, sauté the garlic and onions in a small saucepan for about 5 to 7 minutes till it's tender. Then remove it from the oven.

- Use a bowl to combine the cheese, salt, pepper, parsley, egg whites and garlic. Mix it properly.
- Add the meat and use your hands to gently mix till the mixture is well combined.
- Form the mixture into ¾ ounces-meatballs of 1-inch each, lay these meatballs on a baking sheet and bake for 10 to 15 minutes or till it reaches 160F.
- Remove it from heat, let it cool and then serve.

Nutritional Value

Serving size: about 3 ounces

Cholesterol: 76mg   Calories: 198

Saturated Fat: 4g   Total Fat: 10g

Sodium: 502mg   Monounsaturated Fat: 4g

Total Carbs: 2g   Protein: 26mg

Hawaiian Calzone

Cooking Duration: about 10 mins.

Ingredients

- Chopped Canadian bacon – 4 ounces.
- Chopped green onion – 1

- Medium-sized tomato, chopped – 1.
- Red bell pepper, chopped and roasted – ¼ pepper.
- Crushed and drained pineapples – 1½ tablespoons.
- Fat-free Dijon honey salad dressing – 1 tablespoon.
- Whole wheat bread dough, frozen or refrigerated – 10 ounces
- Shredded mixed cheese (provolone, parmesan, romano and mozzarella) – ¼ cup.
- Olive oil – 1 teaspoon.
- Salt-free tomato sauce – 1 cup.
- Oregano – ½ tablespoon.

Instructions

- Heat the oven to 400 F, thinly coat the baking sheet with cooking spray.
- Mix the bacon, peppers, tomato, pepper and salad dressing in a large bowl. Mix thoroughly.
- Divine the dough into four pieces on a floured surface, mould each piece into a circle.
- Use a roller to roll the dough into an oval shape. Top each oval with 1 tablespoon of cheese and the bacon mixture.
- Fold the dough to contain the filling and press each side, press with a fork and place it on a baking sheet.

- Lightly coat the Calzone with olive oil, bake for about 10 minutes till it is golden brown.
- Top each calzone with a quarter cup of warm tomato sauce, sprinkle oregano and serve at once.

Nutritional Value

Serving size: 1 calzone.

Calories: 303

Total Carbs: 42g

Total Fat: 7g

Saturated Fat: 2g

Cholesterol: 23mg

Protein: 18g

Dietary Fiber: 4g

Total Sugars: 7g

Monounsaturated Fat: 1g

Trans Fat: Trace

Sodium: 717mg

Italian Chicken and Vegetable Packet

Cooking Duration: About 45 mins.

Ingredients

- 3 ounces of Boneless, skinless chicken breast
- ½ cup of Chopped zucchini
- ½ cup of potato (peeled and chopped)
- ¼ cup of Chopped onion
- ¼ cup of Chopped baby carrots
- ¼ cup of Chopped mushrooms
- ¼ teaspoon of Oregano
- 1/8 teaspoon of Garlic powder

Instructions

- Heat the oven to 350 F, cut 12 inches of aluminium foil, fold in

half, unfold then coat the sheet with cooking spray.
- Put the chicken breast on the center of the sheet, top it with potato, onions, zucchini and mushrooms.
- Sprinkle garlic powder and oregano on the vegetables and chicken.
- Bring the foil together, make overlapping folds to seal the foil packet, turn the edges to prevent liquid from escaping while cooking.
- Place the packet on a cookie sheet and bake till vegetables and chicken are tender. This should take about 45 minutes.

Then remove it, remove the foil and serve.

Nutritional Value

Serving size: 1 packet.

Total Fat: 2.5g

Calories: 207

Dietary Fiber: 3g

Trans Fat: Trace

Cholesterol: 62mg

Sodium: 73mg

Saturated Fat: 0.5g

Monounsaturated Fat: 0.5g

Protein: 23g

Total Carbs: 23g

Pork Chops with Blackcurrant Jam Sauce

Total Duration: 7 mins.

Ingredients

- Blackcurrant Jam Sauce – ¼ cup.
- Dijon mustard – 2 tablespoons.
- Olive oil – 2 teaspoons.
- Center-cut pork loin chops, trimmed of all visible fat layers – 6 pieces (4 ounces each).
- Wine vinegar – 1/3 cup.
- Freshly ground black pepper – 1/8 teaspoon.
- Orange slices – 6.

Instructions

- Use a small bowl to mix the jam and mustard, use a large frying

pan to heat the olive oil over fairly high heat.
- Put the pork chops, turning once, giving each side about 5 minutes to get browned. Top each pork chop with a tablespoon of the jam-mustard mixture. Cover and cook for 2 minutes.
- Remove and place in warmed plates.
- Cool the frying pan till it warms, then pour the wine vinegar to remove bits of pork and jam. Pour vinegar sauce onto the pork chop.
- Sprinkle the pepper and use the orange slices to garnish the pork.
- Serve!

Nutritional Value

	Serving size: 1 chop
Protein: 25g	Total Fat: 6g
Cholesterol: 78mg	Calories: 198
Dietary Fiber: 1g	Total Carbs: 11g
Monounsaturated Fat: 3g	
Added Sugars: 8g	Saturated Fat: 1g
Trans Fat: Trace	Sodium: 188mg

Pasta with Pumpkin Sauce

Cooking Duration: 18-20 mins.

Ingredients

- Whole-wheat bow tie pasta – 2 cups.

- Olive oil – 2 teaspoons.
- Medium-sized onion, chopped – 1.
- Minced garlic cloves – 4.
- Sliced, fresh mushrooms – 8 ounces.
- Low-sodium veggie or chicken stock – 1 cup.
- Pumpkin – 1 can (15 ounces).
- Rubbed sage – ½ teaspoon.
- Salt – 1/8 teaspoon.
- Grinded black pepper – ¼ teaspoon.
- Grated parmesan cheese – ¼ cup.
- Dried parsley flakes – 1 tablespoon.

Instructions

- Cook the pasta as directed on the pack.
- Place a large skillet over medium high heat, cook the garlic, mushrooms and onions in the olive oil till the onion is soft. This step should take about 10 minutes.
- Add the stock, salt, pepper and rubbed sage, lower the heat and let it simmer for about 8 minutes.
- When the pasta is boiled, drain and mix it with the pumpkin sauce, stir gently.
- Top the combination with parsley and parmesan cheese. It is ready to be served.

Nutritional Value

Serving size: about 2 cups.

Total Fat: 5g   Calories: 197

Saturated Fat: 2g   Protein: 9g

Monounsaturated Fat: 2g

Total Carbs: 29g   Cholesterol: 4mg

Sodium: 176mg   Dietary Fiber: 5g

Apple Dumplings

Cooking Duration: About 30 mins.

Ingredients

Dough:

- Butter – 1 tablespoon.

- 1 teaspoon of Honey
- 2 tablespoons of Rolled oats
- A cup of Whole-wheat flour
- 2 tablespoons of Buckwheat flour
- 2 tablespoons of Brandy or apple liquor

Apple filling:

- Thin slices of large tart apples – 6 apples.
- Nutmeg – 1 teaspoon.
- Honey – 2 tablespoons.
- Lemon zest – 1 lemon.

Instructions

- Heat the oven to 350 F, then blend butter, honey, oats and

flour in a food processor till the mixture looks perfectly smooth.
- Add the brandy or apple liquor and keep blending till the mixture starts to form a ball.
- Remove the mixture, package it to be airtight in plastic and refrigerate for two hours (this is to be done ahead).
- Mix apple, honey and nutmeg, then lemon zest. Set it apart.
- Roll out the dough on a floured surface to a quarter-inch thickness, cut into 8-inch circles.
- Use an 8-cup muffin, get it coated with cooking spray.
- Place a circle of dough over each cup, gently push the dough

inside the cup, then fill with the apple mixture.
- Fold the sides and pinch it to shut it. Bake at 350 F for about 30 minutes until golden brown.
- Remove and serve.

Nutritional Value

Serving size: 1 dumpling

Total Fat: 2.5g   Calories: 178

Cholesterol: 4mg   Saturated Fat: 1g

Sodium: 14mg   Trans Fat: Trace

Dietary Fiber: 6g   Monounsaturated Fat: 0.5g

Total Carbs: 36g   Added Sugars: 5g

Protein: 3g

Cookies and Cream Shake

Prep Duration: 5-7 mins.

Ingredients

- Chilled Vanilla soy milk – 1 1/3 cups.
- Fat-free Vanilla ice cream – 3 cups.
- Chocolate wafer cookies (crushed) – 6.

Instructions

- Mix the ice cream and soya milk in a blender till the resulting mixture is foamy and smooth.

- Add the chocolate cookies then pulse a few times to blend.
- Turn the mixture into chilled, tall glasses and serve at once.

Nutritional Value

Serving size: 1 cup (full)

Calories: 270　　Total Fat: 3g

Protein: 9g　　Total Carbs: 52g

Saturated Fat: <1g　　Cholesterol: Trace

Dietary Fiber: 11.5g　　Sodium: 229mg

Monounsaturated Fat: <1g

Total sugars: 29g　Added sugars: 11g

Fruit and Nut Bar

Cooking Duration: 20 mins.

Ingredients

- ½ cup of Quinoa flour
- ¼ cup of Chopped dried apricots
- ½ cup of Oats
- ¼ cup of Flaxseed flour
- ¼ cup of dried pineapple (chopped)
- ¼ cup of Wheat germ
- ¼ cup of Chopped almonds
- ¼ cup of Honey
- ¼ cups of Chopped dried figs
- Cornstarch – 2 tablespoons.

Instructions

- Use parchment paper to line a sheet pan.

- Assemble all ingredients and mix well.
- Press the resulting mixture into the pan till it is half an inch-thick.
- Bake it in the oven at a temperature of 300 F for about 20 minutes. Cool completely, cut into 24 pieces then serve.

Nutritional Value

Serving size: 1 bar

Dietary Fiber: 2g	Total Carbs: 11g
Total Fat: 2g	Sodium: 4mg
Saturated Fat: Trace	Protein: 2g
Total sugars: 6g	Monounsaturated Fat: 0.5g
Added sugars: 3g	Calories: 70

Low Carb Crepes (gluten free)

Ingredients

- ¾ cup of almond milk
- 2 tablespoons of flax meal
- 2 tablespoons of coconut floor
- 2 eggs
- 1 tablespoon of coconut oil
- ¼ cup of hemp seeds
- 1 tablespoon of cinnamon
- ¼ cup of apple juice
- A pinch of salt

Instructions

- Add all the ingredients into a magic bullet or a blender and blend until you get a smooth texture. Allow the

batter to rest for about 2 minutes while you get your nonstick pan ready.
- Place the non-stick pan on medium-low heat.
- Once hot, pour in coconut oil or butter and fry the mixture, fry the first side for about 3 minutes then turn to the second side and fry for about a minute.
- Allow to cool off before you serve!

Paleo Cinnamon Apple Crisp

Ingredients

- 2 ½ teaspoon of cinnamon

- 7/8 medium sized organic green Apples
- 2 lemon or limes (juiced out)
- ¼ teaspoon of sea salt
- ¾ cup of pecan halves
- 4 tablespoons of coconut oil or grass-fed unsalted butter
- ¼ cup of honey
- ¾ cup of walnuts halves
- ½ cup of coconut shreds
- 1 tablespoon of honey for topping

Instructions

- Peel the apples and slice into bits then mix with the lime/ lemon extracts. Cinnamon and melted honey.

- Place the apples in an oval glass baking tray.
- Heat the butter, nuts, sea salt, coconut shreds and a tablespoon of honey until they all mix together.
- Use a spoon to spread the topping equally on the apple.
- Heat up your oven on 350 degree then put the baking tray to bake for approximately 30 minutes.
- Remove the cover and return back to the oven for another 30 minutes.

Instructions for the Whipping Cream

- Simply whip a cold heavy whipping cream using your electric mixer for approximately 5 minutes to get it stiffened.

- Use it as a topping on the Cinnamon Apple Crisp.

Paleo Banana Bread Recipe

Ingredients

- ¼ cup of flaxseed meal
- 1 teaspoon of baking powder
- 2 cups of almond flour
- 1 teaspoon of baking powder
- 4 overripe bananas
- 2/3 cup of chopped nuts
- 1 teaspoon of vanilla extract
- 4 eggs
- 2 tablespoons of local honey

Instructions

- Heat up the oven to 375 degrees F.
- Sort your dry ingredients in a big bowl.
- Add the eggs, mashed bananas, vanilla and honey in a different bowl and mix together.
- Dig a small hole in the dry ingredients and pour the wet ingredients into the hole. Mix together as you desire.
- Grease your baking cups, muffin tins, big load pans or mini loaf pans.
- Then full the pan up to 3/4 inches.
- Put in the oven to bake for about 22 to 25 minutes for the muffin while the loaves bake for approximately 30 minutes or until you can insert a

toothpick into the bread and it comes out clean.
- Take out of the oven and keep aside to cool off steam.
- Enjoy with your grass-fed butter or almond butter.

Paleo Pumpkin Bars with Coconut Flour

Ingredients

- ¼ cup of coconut oil
- 1 teaspoon of baking soda
- 5 eggs
- ½ cup of coconut flour
- 1 cup of pumpkin puree
- ½ teaspoon of cinnamon

- ¼ teaspoon of cloves
- ¼ cup of real maple syrup
- A dash of ginger
- ½ teaspoon of nutmeg
- 1 teaspoon of vanilla (optional)

Instructions

- Heat up oven to 400-degree F.
- Add all the ingredients into your mixer and mix until all is well mixed. The batter should be thick at this point
- Evenly spread it on an 8 by 8 pan that has been previously oiled or has parchment paper placed on.
- Put in the oven to bake for about 15 to 20 minutes or until when the top

turns slightly brown and the middle is set.
- Serve!

Honey Graham Cracker Pie Crust

Ingredients

- 1 egg
- ¼ teaspoon of salt
- ¼ cup of almond flour
- 1 teaspoon of cinnamon
- ¼ teaspoon of baking soda
- ½ cup and 2 tablespoons of coconut flour
- ¼ cup of honey
- ¼ cup of coconut oil, softened
- 1 teaspoon of vanilla

Instructions

- Heat up oven to 350 degrees.
- Add all the dry ingredients into a bowl and mix together
- Add all the wet ingredients into a different bowl and mix together.
- Add the wet ingredients into the bowl of dry ingredients.
- Use your fingers to spread the dough equally in a tart pan or a 9-inch pie pan.
- If using a pie pan, allow it to bake for approximately 15 minutes and 7 minutes to bake if using a tart pan.
- If your filling does not require baking, take out of the oven, allow to cool down before you add the filling.

- If you want to bake the filling, allow the crust to bake for about 5 to 7 minutes or until it turns light golden.
- Put the crust in the freezer for approximately 30 minutes then add the filling and put back into the oven.
- You may cover the sides to avoid it getting burnt easily.

Chapter 5

Conclusion

Prediabetes is the ultimate warning sign or symptom for the dreaded diabetes. As long as individuals pay attention to their blood sugar level by dieting, engaging in physical exercises and changes in lifestyle (reducing smoking or stopping it altogether and drinking moderately), Prediabetes can be prevented, controlled or reversed.

This book contains factual knowledge on the causes, symptoms, myths, treatment and diet plans for the condition. This same knowledge is not limited to people living with Prediabetes and type 2 Diabetes. It also extends to non-diabetics as well.

Included also, the main part of this book, are the recipes for the various healthy meals that can control the blood sugar level and keep it at a healthy level.

Other Books by Nancy Peterson

- CELERY JUICE: The Natural Medicine for Healing Your Body and Weight Loss (Contains Secret Celery Recipes) https://amzn.to/2xTTC4Z

- LOW CARB DIET FOOD LIST: Best Foods to Eat on a Low Carb Diet Along with a Meal Plan, for Healthy Living and Weight Loss https://amzn.to/2JuxxjR

- ENDOMORPH DIET PLAN: The Complete Guide to Loss that Excess Fat and Stay Healthy with Paleo Diet, Exercises and Trainings Perfect for Your Body Type. Includes

Recipes and Meal Plan

https://amzn.to/2xNU3NW

Made in United States
Troutdale, OR
05/17/2024